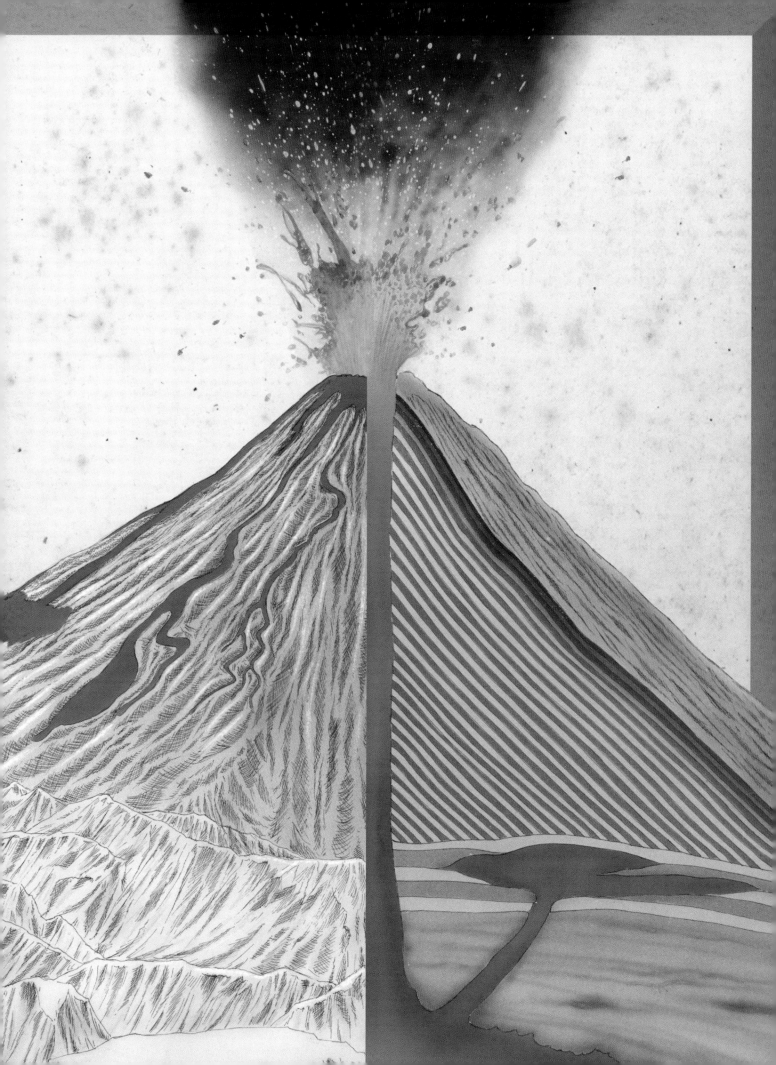

Published by Smart Apple Media,
an imprint of Black Rabbit Books
P.O. Box 3263, Mankato, Minnesota 56002
www.blackrabbitbooks.com

Published by arrangement with
The Salariya Book Company Ltd

Cataloging-in-Publication Data is available
from the Library of Congress

Printed in the United States
At Corporate Graphics,
North Mankato, Minnesota

9 8 7 6 5 4 3 2 1

ISBN: 978-1-62588-342-1

Illustrators: Nicholas Hewetson
                 David Antram

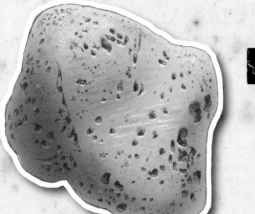

VOLCANOES

John Cooper

A⁺

Smart Apple Media

Hot Earth

arth is a hot planet. Most of this heat comes from the Sun, and if we could trap all the sunlight falling on Earth in one day, we would have enough heat and energy to last for the next century. But Earth also produces heat. Usually we only notice this if we live near a volcano, hot springs, or geysers, or if we experience an earthquake or tsunami. From its beginnings, over 4.6 billion years ago, Earth has from time to time unleashed the huge forces contained beneath its surface.

geyser

Timeline

FACTFILE
HOT EARTH

• Hot rocks near the surface heat water that seeps into the soil. As more water seeps in, the hot water rises. It boils at the surface to form a hot spring, or a mud pot if the water is muddy.

• Temperatures within Earth can reach 2,730°F (1,500°C)—and rocks melt. Volcanoes occur when the huge pressure within Earth causes molten rock to erupt onto its surface.

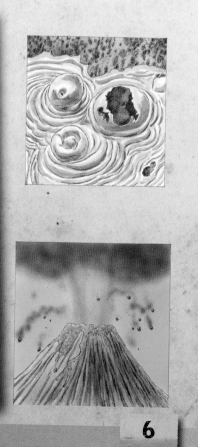

◀ Geysers are hot springs. Deep underground, hot water collects under increasing pressure until it erupts at high speed to form a geyser. As fresh water collects it erupts again and again. Old Faithful in the Yellowstone National Park, Wyoming, erupts every 65 or 91 minutes or so, 24 hours a day. Its water spout can reach a height of 183 feet (56 m).

Volcanoes

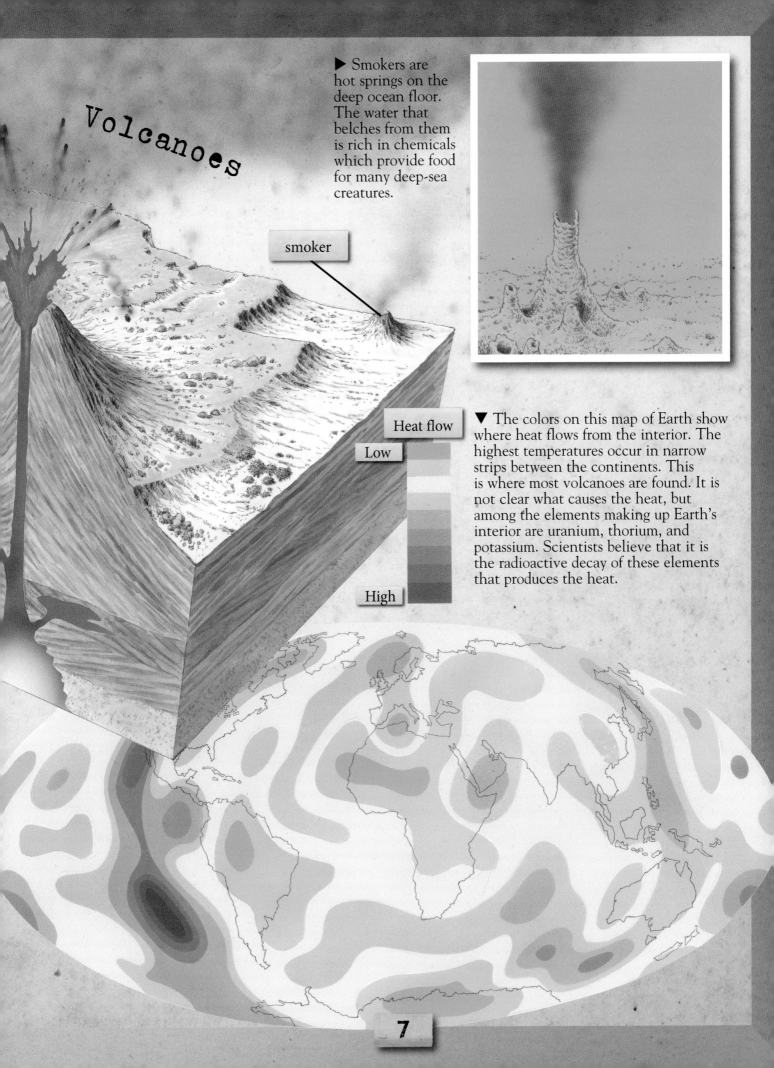

▶ Smokers are hot springs on the deep ocean floor. The water that belches from them is rich in chemicals which provide food for many deep-sea creatures.

smoker

Heat flow

Low

High

▼ The colors on this map of Earth show where heat flows from the interior. The highest temperatures occur in narrow strips between the continents. This is where most volcanoes are found. It is not clear what causes the heat, but among the elements making up Earth's interior are uranium, thorium, and potassium. Scientists believe that it is the radioactive decay of these elements that produces the heat.

We may have explored Earth's surface, but we know little about what is under its crust. Earthquakes give scientists the best clues to work out Earth's structure. Earthquakes create shock waves like ripples in a pond. Scientists use seismometers to measure the waves as they travel. The waves vary according to what they pass through; this allows scientists to build up a picture of what is inside Earth.

▼ Earth's surface, or crust, is not solid. It consists of "plates" floating on a liquid mantle. The hot mantle rocks push out along ridges in the middle of the oceans to form undersea volcanoes and new crust. Forced outward, the plates grind together and create earthquakes and volcanoes.

▼ Plates at the ocean's edges are forced down into the mantle. This can push up the land to form mountains. The Andes and Rockies are being pushed up along the west coast of South and North America.

inner core

Volcanoes form at a mid-ocean ridge, where Earth's surface keeps moving apart. The mantle rises toward the surface and the release of pressure pushes magma through cracks in the rock.

Mid-ocean volcanoes form over "hot spots." These are areas of Earth's surface where active centers within the mantle cause magma to rise. They occur on the ocean floor and on land.

An ocean plate dips below the continent, forming a deep ocean trench. The plate pushing slowly down into Earth causes earthquakes and volcanic activity.

New ocean plates spread out on each side of the ridge.

crust

mantle

outer
core

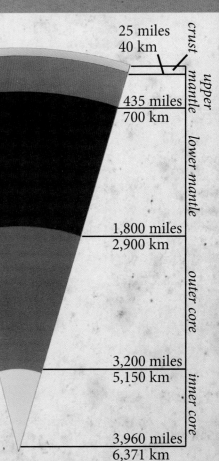

25 miles
40 km

crust

upper mantle

435 miles
700 km

lower mantle

1,800 miles
2,900 km

outer core

3,200 miles
5,150 km

inner core

3,960 miles
6,371 km

FACTFILE
EARTH'S LAYERS

• Earth's surface layer is called the crust. Under the oceans the crust is around 6 miles (10 km) thick, but beneath land it can be up to 25 miles (40 km) thick.

• The mantle below the crust is about 1,800 miles (2,900 km) deep.

• Earth's central core has two parts: a large outer liquid one, and a small inner one which is believed to be made of the metals iron and nickel.

Mountains and Volcanoes

As the ocean plate goes under the continental plate into the mantle, it makes the land "wrinkle" and form mountains. The ocean plate is melted by the mantle and turns into magma.

Friction between ocean and continental plates melts rock and produces more volcanoes.

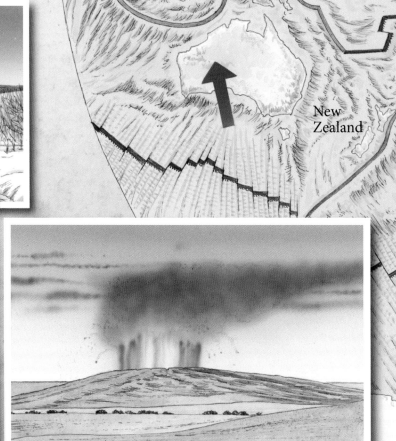

New Zealand

FACTFILE
SHIELD VOLCANOES

Shield volcanoes, like those in the Hawaiian islands, form low, rather flat mountains. Huge quantities of runny lava spread out quickly, usually from long cracks rather than single craters. Shield volcanoes rarely erupt with big explosions or ash clouds. They are common under the sea, often near the

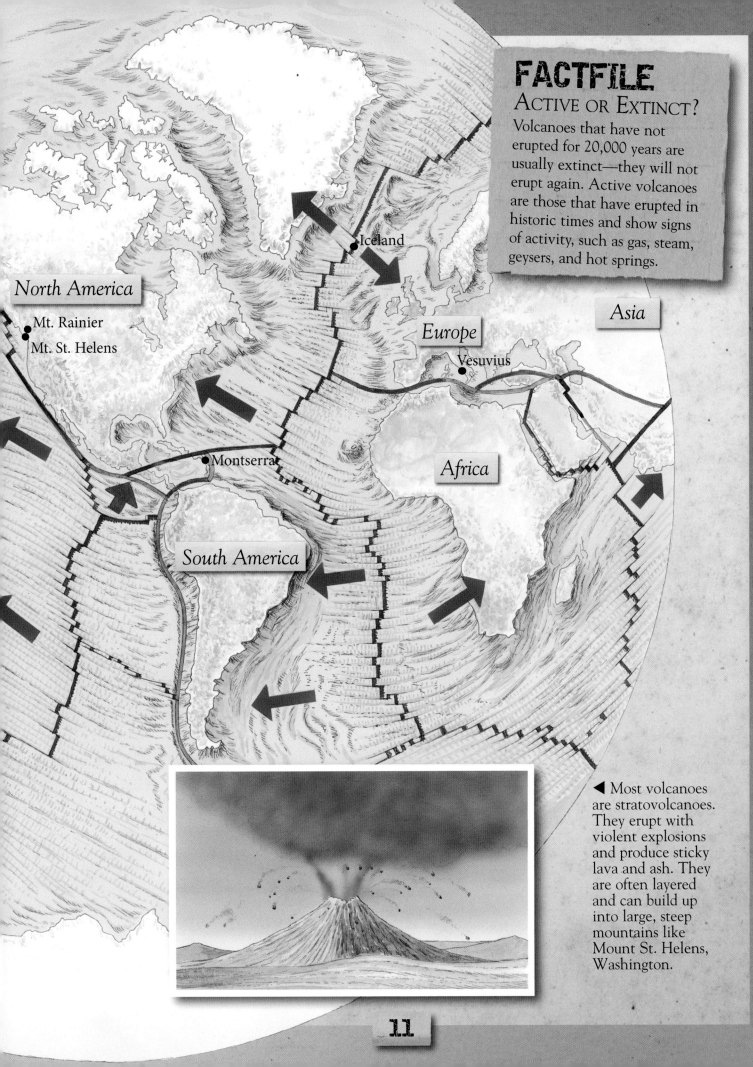

North America

Mt. Rainier
Mt. St. Helens

Montserrat

South America

Iceland

Europe

Vesuvius

Africa

Asia

FACTFILE

ACTIVE OR EXTINCT?
Volcanoes that have not
erupted for 20,000 years are
usually extinct—they will not
erupt again. Active volcanoes
are those that have erupted in
historic times and show signs
of activity, such as gas, steam,
geysers, and hot springs.

◄ Most volcanoes
are stratovolcanoes.
They erupt with
violent explosions
and produce sticky
lava and ash. They
are often layered
and can build up
into large, steep
mountains like
Mount St. Helens,
Washington.

▼ Volcanic dust in Earth's atmosphere can cause dramatic sunsets. When Krakatau, in Indonesia, erupted in 1883, dust circulated for two years. Volcanic dust can make Earth's temperature fall.

▼ Really big explosions can send a column of dust and gases many miles into the atmosphere at speeds of 1,640 feet (500 m) per second. The larger particles soon fall, but the volcanic dust can be blown all around the world.

▲ Ash and rocks, the crushed remains of the volcano's dome, explode into the air. Most fall close to the volcano and, with every eruption, make the volcano higher and higher.

▶ Volcanoes spew out magma, gases, ash, dust, and rocks. The magma (known as lava once it is out of the ground) flows down the sides of the volcano from the central crater, or from vents in the sides.

lava, each
mpostion.
ent in lava.
contains a
led andesite
olcanic glass,
very quickly.

and can be
ry sharp
dians and
ri peoples
ds and
used it for
is mirror.

◀ Basalt is lava which cooled slowly. It often forms large, straight-sided columns. The Giant's Causeway in Northern Ireland is a famous example.

▶ Large lumps of molten lava may be hurled from a volcano. As it speeds through the air, the lava is shaped into a smooth, tear-shaped "bomb" before it solidifies. If the lava is very runny, small lumps are drawn out into really long, thin strands. These are called "Pelé's Hair" after the Hawaiian goddess of volcanoes.

Pelé

▼ Sometimes volcanoes produce pasty lava with a lot of gas in it. The gas appears as bubbles—a sort of volcanic froth. It cools very quickly to form pumice, a pale, light rock, and one of the very few rocks that float.

◀ Runny lava has little silica in it and flows faster than pasty lava. Runny lava forms basalt when it cools. Repeated surges of lava on the ocean floor build up to form what is termed pillow lava.

FACTFILE

SULFUR

Sulfur is one of the commonest minerals produced by volcanoes. It sometimes forms beautiful yellow crystals, but usually occurs in shapeless masses around volcanic vents. It is used to make sulfuric acid and in making matches, fireworks, and gunpowder.

Sulfur crystals

Volcanoes in Europe

etween the two great plates of Earth's crust that carry the continents of Asia and Europe is a volcanic danger zone. In this zone are the countries of Turkey, Greece, the former Yugoslavia, Italy, and France, and the Mediterranean Sea. Iceland is over the mid-ocean ridge of the North Atlantic, an area of high volcanic activity.

▼ Santorini, a group of islands in the Mediterranean, forms a broken circle.

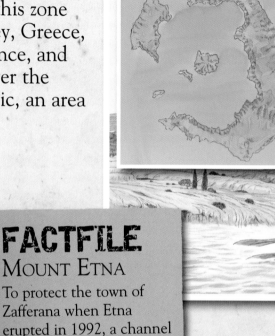

The European volcanic zone

Grímsvötn, Iceland

Mt. Etna, Sicily, Italy

Santorini, Greece

FACTFILE
MOUNT ETNA
To protect the town of Zafferana when Etna erupted in 1992, a channel was dug for the lava to flow into and cool safely.

◀ Etna has a long history of eruptions. The earliest known took place in 1500 BCE. It has erupted 190 times since then.

◢ Mount Etna is the mythical home of Vulcan, the Roman fire god, from whose name the word *volcano* comes.

◀ The islands of Santorini are the remains of a huge collapsed crater, or *caldera*. There have been at least 12 massive explosions here in the last 200,000 years. These islands were formed in 1650 BCE by the largest explosion on Earth in 10,000 years.

The volcano of Grímsvötn is below Iceland's thick ice cap. In 1996 an earthquake below the ice heralded the start of an eruption. Next day there were large cracks in the glaciers and by the third day there was a crater 5 miles (9 km) long filled with meltwater. Seventeen days later a wall of water 30 feet (9 m) high poured out. Fortunately, the water drained into the sea.

▶ The island of Surtsey appeared off the coast of Iceland in 1963—the result of an eruption 425 feet (130 m) below the surface of the sea. The magma's reaction with the seawater caused spectacular explosions. Eruptions continued for more than three years.

Uni

In 19
it wo
were
was
8.2
dis
(2

FACTFILE
MONTSERRAT

- Ash from Soufrière Hills in Montserrat has landed on the islands of Nevis and Antigua, 25 miles (40 km) away.
- Each eruption pumps up to 770 U.S. tons (700 metric tons) of sulfur dioxide into the atmosphere.
- Two-thirds of the island is now uninhabitable.

▶ On July 18, 1995, on the Caribbean island of Montserrat, the Soufrière Hills volcano began to send up steam and ash.

The Soufrière Hills volcano has been erupting on and off since 1995, most recently in February 2010. Small earthquakes, gas, ash, and columns of dust thousands of miles high accompany the eruptions.

▲ Mount Rainier in Washington may be the most dangerous volcano in the United States. It has not erupted for over 2,000 years, but is near a large center of population.

 round the Pacific Ocean is the "ring of fire"—the zone with most of the world's active volcanoes. In the Pacific itself, most of the islands were formed by eruptions. There are even more active volcanoes under the Pacific Ocean than there are on land.

Hawaiian Islands

Midway Islands
28 million years old

Kauai
5.1 million years old

Motion of Pacific Plate

Maui
1.3 million years old

Hawaii
800,000 years old

Hawaiian Ridge

▶ The volcanic Hawaiian islands are over a hot spot —a permanent source of magma deep in Earth's mantle. A volcano grows over the hot spot, then, as the Pacific plate moves on, a new volcano grows in its place, forming a chain of islands. Hawaii is the most recent island. A new island will appear eventually when Loihi, an undersea volcano southeast of Kilauea, erupts above sea level.

Mauna Kea is the tallest volcano on Hawaii at 13,796 feet (4,205 m). If its height is measured from the sea floor, it is 5.5 miles (9 km) high, making it the tallest mountain on Earth. It last erupted about 3,500 years ago and is thought to be dormant. Mauna Loa, also on Hawaii, is Earth's largest volcano. The 800,000-year-old Kilauea is the island's youngest volcano and is one of the most active on Earth.

Hawaiian Islands

Midway Islands

Kauai

Hawaii

▲ There are more than 30 volcanoes in Japan but the most famous is Mount Fuji with its symmetrical snow-capped peak. Mount Fuji is about 60 miles (100 km) from Tokyo and rises 12,388 feet (3,776 m) above the low-lying plain. It last erupted over 300 years ago but it is still active. It has erupted 16 times since 781 CE, and there were two very large eruptions in 1050 BCE and 930 BCE.

FACTFILE
PACIFIC VOLCANOES

In the warm Pacific Ocean, coral reefs grow around the volcanic islands (a). Over millions of years, the volcanoes are worn away and the sea level rises (b). The coral continues to grow upward and forms an atoll—a ring of small coral islands around a central lagoon (c).

▶ The two islands of New Zealand lie where two of Earth's crustal plates meet. The Pacific plate is disappearing under the Indian–Australian plate. As a result, New Zealand has the highest number of recent volcanoes in the world, and large numbers of geysers and hot springs.

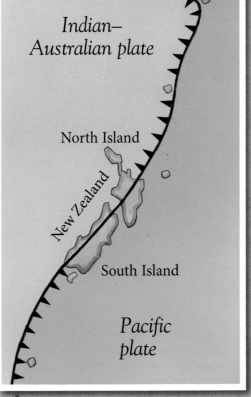

Indian–Australian plate

North Island

New Zealand

South Island

Pacific plate

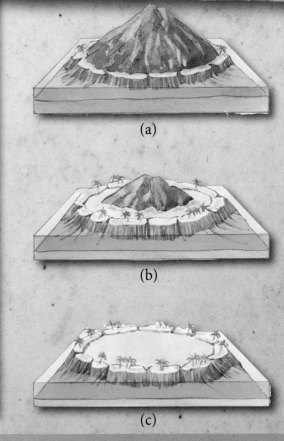

(a)

(b)

(c)

Historic Disasters

Vesuvius
79 CE

▲ At least 2,000 people living in nearby Pompeii died, overcome by poisonous gases and suffocating ash. Archaeologists uncovered body-shaped cavities which reveal the moments of death. About 10 feet (3 m) of ash fell on the town. Herculaneum, west of Vesuvius, was buried under 75 feet (23 m) of ash. Most of its population of 5,000 escaped before the eruption.

▲ The historian Pliny the Younger watched Vesuvius erupt and destroy both Pompeii and Herculaneum. In a letter to his friend Tacitus he described the earthquakes, the eruption, the lava flows, and the huge ash cloud, as well as the destruction and the death toll.

This dog, chained to a post and unable to flee, was suffocated by the ash.

FACTFILE
VESUVIUS

Vesuvius, a stratovolcano, is at least 300,000 years old. It is still deadly: in 1631 mudflows and lava killed 3,500 people.

olcanoes have been erupting ever since our planet formed. Many early peoples must have seen catastrophic explosions, but left no records of them. The eruption of Vesuvius in 79 CE was the first to be described in detail. For clues as to what happened before that date, geologists have to study rocks.

Mount Pelée

◀ Mount Pelée on the island of Martinique is famous for the eruption which killed up to 40,000 people in 1902. A *nuée ardente*—a lethal, glowing hot ash cloud that hugs the ground and travels at high speed—destroyed everything in its path, including the city of St. Pierre.

◀ One person survived—a prisoner in jail. He was badly burned, but the thick walls protected him from the worst of the eruption.

Verlaten

Lang

The rest of Krakatau before August 26, 1883

Krakatau

◀ Krakatau in Indonesia was one of three islands that formed the remains of a caldera about 4 miles (7 km) wide. In May 1883 it began to erupt. In August, what is believed to to be the loudest explosion ever heard shook the island and two-thirds of it vanished. The eruption caused a huge tsunami 130 feet (40 m) high, killing 36,000 people on neighboring islands.

Earthquakes are the biggest threat because they cannot be predicted. Volcanic eruptions can now be predicted quite accurately. They may cause damage to buildings or to electricity, gas, and water supplies, but cause little loss of life. But eruptions like that of Mount Pinatubo in the Philippines, in 1991, can cause widespread economic disaster.

▼ In 1991 a long-expected eruption blasted off the top 490 feet (150 m) of Mount Pinatubo. Downpours of rain mixed with ash to form mud torrents, or *lahars*. 900 people died, 110,000 homes were destroyed, and 1.2 million lives were disrupted, but the early prediction saved lives.

FACTFILE
MOUNT PINATUBO

- Mount Pinatubo has erupted many times since it formed 35,000 years ago.
- The dust cloud caused by the 1991 eruption and the vast amount of sulfur dioxide it sent into the atmosphere caused world temperatures to fall.

▼ In 1973 the volcano Helgafell, on the Icelandic island of Heimaey, started to erupt. Lava began to fill the streets and destroy houses in the town of Vestmannaeyjar. Most of the residents were evacuated. The lava threatened to destroy the harbor, so the remaining islanders began pumping seawater onto the lava to cool it. The plan worked: the cooled lava gradually slowed and the harbor was saved.

The eruption of Mount Pinatubo caused damage to roads, bridges, and homes that would take years to repair. Damage to the economy of the Philippines is impossible to calculate.

◄ Mount Pinatubo's eruption, combined with later typhoons, caused lahars, or mud torrents. This dam built in a gorge was overcome by the lahars, which scoured out the 60-foot-deep (18-m) channel below.

FACTFILE
HELGAFELL

The 1973 eruption on Heimaey formed a new volcanic cone. Now 915 feet (279 m) high, it is called Eldfell (fire mountain).

◄ In 2011 an earthquake shook Japan. The tsunami that followed killed 18,000 people. Many towns were flattened by waves that reached 130 feet (29 m) high and traveled up to 6 miles (10 km) inland in places.

Volcanoes in Time and Space

ince Earth formed, 4.6 billion years ago, volcanoes have helped shape its surface. Volcanic rocks have been found in areas where there is no activity today. Huge lava flows in India dating from 65 million years ago perhaps helped wipe out the dinosaurs. There are also volcanic remains in Scotland and Northern Ireland. Space exploration has now shown that volcanoes also occur on other planets.

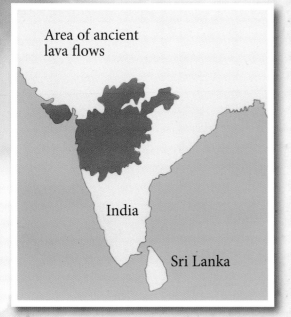

Area of ancient
lava flows

India

Sri Lanka

◀ Vast eruptions in India produced huge quantities of gas and lava, perhaps causing temperatures to drop too low for dinosaurs to survive.

▶ Devil's Tower in Wyoming is believed to be the result of underground volcanic activity about 50 million years ago.

Olympus Mons

Mount Everest

Mauna Kea

Width of Olympus Mons

Width of Grand Canyon

▲ Olympus Mons on Mars is huge: the volcano is about 16 miles (25 km) high and 336 miles (540 km) wide. Here it is compared with large natural features on Earth.

▼ Earth is not the only volcanic planet in the solar system. Venus has the most volcanoes, with over 1,600 volcanoes or volcanic features visible from space. Mars and the Moon both have some volcanic features which are believed to be ancient. Io, one of the moons that orbit Jupiter, is the most volcanically active body in the entire solar system. Eruptions on its surface have been photographed by passing spacecraft.

◄ The temperature of lava is measured by inserting a type of thermometer, a thermocouple, into it. In this way temperatures up to 2,120°F (1,160°C) can be recorded. If the temperatures are higher, special equipment is used at a safe distance from the lava.

◄ Volcanic gases can be measured with a spectrometer, a piece of equipment sensitive enough to analyze gas from a distance of more than half a mile (1 km). Many volcanoes produce about 190 U.S. tons (170 metric tons) of sulfuric acid a day.

FACTFILE
PACIFIC VOLCANOES
Photographs and films are the closest most of us get to active volcanoes. But getting a good shot is dangerous. In 1991, husband and wife team Maurice and Katia Krafft were killed filming an eruption.

Volcano Quiz

1. What is Old Faithful in the Yellowstone National Park, Wyoming?
   a) A volcano
   b) A geyser
   c) A hot spring

2. What is the zone containing volcanoes which surrounds the Pacific Ocean called?
   a) The fire zone
   b) The fiery ring
   c) The ring of fire

3. The Giant's Causeway, Northern Ireland, is made of which type of volcanic rock?
   a) Basalt
   b) Andesite
   c) Granite

4. Which new island formed off the coast of Iceland in 1963?
   a) Crete
   b) Surtsey
   c) Heimaey

5. What is the name of the Caribbean island which has erupted most recently?
   a) Montserrat
   b) Martinique
   c) Antigua

6. Which Hawaiian volcano is the world's largest?
   a) Kilauea
   b) Mauna Kea
   c) Mauna Loa

7. Which volcanic eruption was the first to be described in recorded history?
   a) Krakatau
   b) Vesuvius
   c) Santorini

8. On which body in the solar system has an erupting volcano been photographed?
   a) Mars
   b) Io
   c) Venus

9. What instrument is used to record the temperature of lava?
   a) Thermocouple
   b) Spectrometer
   c) Seismometer

10. Which mineral with yellow crystals is produced by volcanoes and hot springs?
    a) Pumice
    b) Obsidian
    c) Sulfur

Quiz answers

1) b   see page 6
2) c   see page 10
3) a   see page 15
4) b   see page 17
5) a   see page 19
6) c   see page 20
7) b   see page 23
8) b   see page 27
9) a   see page 29
10) c   see page 15

30

Glossary

active volcano A volcano that shows signs of activity, even if it has not erupted recently.

andesite Volcanic rock, rich in silica, named after the Andes mountains in South America.

basalt Volcanic rock not so rich in silica, usually very dark in color.

caldera A large volcanic crater, usually formed by the collapse of a volcano from below.

carbon dioxide A common gas which all animals produce in small quantities, and volcanoes in large quantities. Too much carbon dioxide in Earth's atmosphere affects the climate.

core Earth's central layer.

crater The hole in the top of a volcano from which the main eruptions occur.

crust The layer of rocks that covers Earth's surface, both on land and under the sea.

dome The swollen top of a volcano before it erupts, usually with massive explosions.

dormant volcano A volcano that has not erupted for many thousands of years, but could become active at any time.

earthquake A violent shaking of the ground, often associated with volcanic explosions.

extinct volcano One that has not erupted for many thousands of years and is unlikely to do so again.

geologist A scientist who studies rocks.

geyser An eruption of superheated water from underground cavities close to hot volcanic rocks.

hot springs Pools of hot water that gather where superheated water from deep underground mixes with colder ground water.

hydrogen sulfide Poisonous and smelly gas given off during volcanic eruptions.

lahar Extremely destructive mudflow caused when a sudden release of water down a volcano's side mixes with earth, ash, and rocks. The water may come from a crater lake or from melting snow and ice.

lava Molten or liquid rock that flows from volcanoes at very high temperatures.

magma Molten rock held deep underground in Earth's mantle.

mantle The part of Earth which is between the crust and the core.

mud pot Similar to a hot spring, but occurring where the ground is very muddy.

nuée ardente A lethal, fast-moving flow of hot gas and ash. The name is French and means "glowing cloud."

pillow lava Lava that has erupted underwater and forms "pillow" shapes as each small flow of lava cools quickly on the outside to form a skin. This skin then bursts, which allows more lava to escape.

plates The sections into which the rocks of Earth's crust are divided.

radioactive Rocks are radioactive when atoms in the elements they contain decay and are released, often as heat. The rate of this decay can be measured and gives valuable scientific information.

rhyolite A sticky type of lava rich in silica.

seismometer An instrument which measures the shock waves in the Earth created by earthquakes.

shield volcano A type of volcano that erupts runny lava, which eventually forms a low, flat cone known as a "shield."

silica A mineral which is very common in rocks and which is always present in lava, in greater or lesser amounts.

smoker A hot spring on the seabed.

stratovolcano A type of volcano that builds up into a steep-sided cone, often with alternating layers of ash and lava.

sulfur dioxide Poisonous gas, often associated with volcanic explosions.

tsunami A huge wave (sometimes called a tidal wave) caused by massive volcanic eruptions and earthquakes under the ocean far from land. When they reach land, such waves often devastate coastal areas.

vents Holes in the sides of volcanoes out of which the lava flows. A single volcano may have several vents.

vulcanologist A scientist who studies volcanoes.